Introduction

The medieval period was a fascinating time in British history. The landscape changed dramatically with the building of huge castles to control the land.Young noblemen learned the rules of chivalry and trained to become knights. The church became very powerful and even kings feared it. The Church financed the building of magnificent cathedrals and it was at the centre of art and learning.

Most people were farmers who endured a hard life working on land owned by nobleman, who in turn owed service to the King. It was a very bloody period with wars against the Irish, Welsh and Scots and a long war with France. There were crusades to the Holy Land and powerful lords fought each other to gain power, or the throne of England.

Our book begins at the time of the Norman conquest of England and ends at the start of the Tudor monarchy, with the defeat of Richard III by Henry VII at the Battle of Bosworth.

Contents

Written & illustrated by William Webb
Front cover illustration by Les Ives

Print reference number 37384/12/11

Norman Britain

The last Saxon king, Harold, was killed at the Battle of Hastings in 1066. The victor was a distant relative of the English royal family and a French nobleman, Duke William 'the Bastard' of Normandy. Long after his death he became known as 'The Conqueror'.

After his victory William expected the Saxon nobles to proclaim him king, but they did not. So he marched his army to London, destroying the countryside on his way. He gave the Saxon lands belonging to those who had opposed him to his Norman supporters. He built wooden castles to keep an iron grip on his conquest, many of which were re-built in stone. The Tower of London (right) was probably the first stone 'keep' to be built in England. William was crowned king in Westminster Abbey on Christmas Day, 1066.

The Domesday Book

In 1086 William ordered a national survey of land distribution, livestock and people in every county. This meant he could tax people more efficiently and settle quarrels over land ownership. The Domesday Book took less than nine months to complete and today it tells historians a great deal about Norman England.

Feudal Society

The lower Anglo-Saxon classes were slaves, but in Europe they no longer had slaves. William brought 'Feudalism' to England, whereby a man worked and lived on the land owned by a lord, bishop or abbot of the church. In return for the land the farmers, or 'villeins' paid rent in crops, eggs, meat or money and they fought for their lord if necessary. The lord, or churchman, owed the King for the land they had been given and they paid by fighting for him and supplying him with armed knights. A later king, Henry I, changed this payment to money. Even William, who held land in France, owed service to the French king.

A Villein's Life

The villeins came under the protection of their lord and could only be lawfully punished or executed. Social life centred on church festivals, which often coincided with ancient pre-Christian festivals. They enjoyed a small amount of hawking or hunting, watching tournaments, skating in cold weather, archery, wrestling, stone-throwing, leaping contests, chess, bear-baiting and cock-fighting.

Britain Under Norman Control

William fought off Welsh attacks and made the Scottish King Malcolm Canmore swear loyalty to him. Later the Normans invaded Ireland. The rebellions in the north of England and the threat of an invasion by the Danes caused the King to be particularly ruthless. He adopted a 'scorched earth' policy, ordering his men to destroy every living thing. By 1086 only two Saxon barons remained in control of important English lands and only one Saxon Bishop, Wulfstan, the Bishop of Worcester.

Norman Changes

The Normans introduced 'Romanesque' architecture with elaborately decorated archways. Almost every village had a new stone church where a school was held in the porch. They kept lower Saxon officials in their positions and English law was retained. If you wished to move up in Norman society, you adopted a Norman name. Even though French was spoken by the nobility, the Anglo-Saxon language did not die and was enriched by French words, becoming the English language we know today.

POO!

At William's funeral in Normandy the monks wanted to lower his body into a stone coffin, but the coffin was too small and his body broke open when they tried to force it in. It caused such a bad smell that the service had to be ended quickly!

Did You Know?

William's men probably brought the parts for a 'DIY' wooden castle kit from Normandy in their boats. They would have been able to assemble a fort quickly when they landed in England.

Norman Castles

The first Norman forts were 'motte and bailey' castles made of wood, which could be assembled in two weeks. The motte was an earth mound surrounded by a ditch, which had a wooden or stone tower on top. This made a good high point and the last refuge during an attack. A fine example of a motte can be seen at Pleshey Castle in Essex. At the foot of the motte was the 'bailey', which was a fenced area surrounded by a ditch and bank. This contained the kitchens, hall, chapel, stables, blacksmith's and stores, which were built of wood with wattle and daub walls. The way to get in was across a drawbridge and through a fortified gatehouse.

The Norman knight wore a coat of mail, or 'hauberk', which was made from as many as 30,000 metal rings. His helmet, or 'spangenhelm', was beaten from one piece of metal.

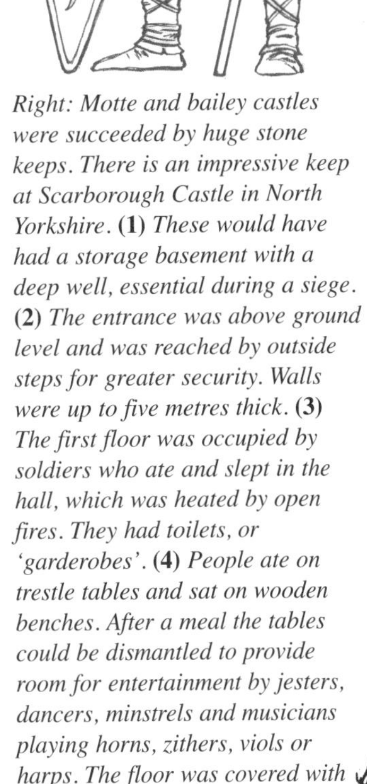

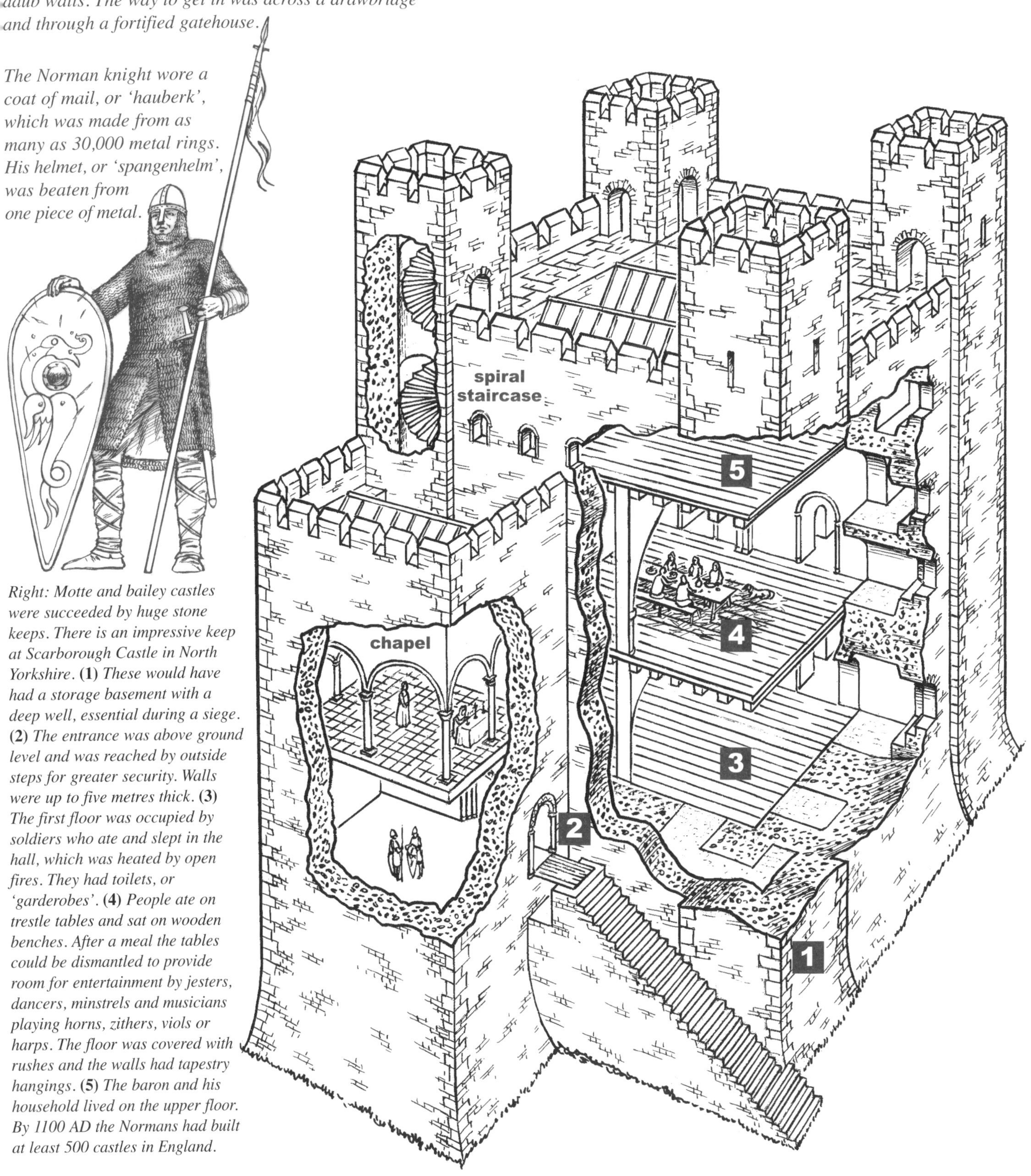

Right: Motte and bailey castles were succeeded by huge stone keeps. There is an impressive keep at Scarborough Castle in North Yorkshire. **(1)** *These would have had a storage basement with a deep well, essential during a siege.* **(2)** *The entrance was above ground level and was reached by outside steps for greater security. Walls were up to five metres thick.* **(3)** *The first floor was occupied by soldiers who ate and slept in the hall, which was heated by open fires. They had toilets, or 'garderobes'.* **(4)** *People ate on trestle tables and sat on wooden benches. After a meal the tables could be dismantled to provide room for entertainment by jesters, dancers, minstrels and musicians playing horns, zithers, viols or harps. The floor was covered with rushes and the walls had tapestry hangings.* **(5)** *The baron and his household lived on the upper floor. By 1100 AD the Normans had built at least 500 castles in England.*

The Age of Chivalry

The polite English gentleman who says 'ladies first' and who believes in 'fair play', whether playing a game or fighting a war, took his manners from the medieval knight's code of chivalry, which came from France with the Normans.

Anyone who owned a certain amount of land had to render service as a knight. Originally any nobleman could make someone a knight, but later this duty could only be performed by the King. Knighthoods finally became limited to a few nobles, who were part of the royal court.

By the 13th century knights had adopted heraldic symbols on their shields, banners and clothing. The typical knight had to be a skilled fighter, amusing, well-mannered and able to romance a lady. The legendary story of King Arthur became the Christian ideal of knighthood.

A Lady

The idea of 'courtly love' came from France, along with poems, ballads and manuals about the art of love. The knight's lady gave strength to him in war. He wore her token, which might be a stocking, when riding into battle. She would be his riding companion, play chess or backgammon with him and bring him comfort when he was weary or wounded. However, many marriages were arranged and a noblewoman's daily duties did not leave her with much time for romance. She taught her own children and those from nearby noble houses and often ran the castle and estate in her husband's absence.

Design a medieval costume for a lady and colour it in. Don't forget to create an unusual headpiece with patterns, jewels and some silk hangings.

Tournaments

When he was not at war, the knight was able to continue his fighting in tournaments. Originally the tournaments were fights between large groups of knights, but they were so dangerous that King Henry II banned them. By the 14th century these battles had become more like exercises in chivalry between knights and were bound by special rules. Knights also enjoyed hunting and hawking.

War

The code of chivalry extended to war, which was often an extremely bloody affair. There were rules about the surrender of towns, the capture of prisoners and other aspects of warfare. However, civilians and ordinary soldiers did not benefit from these rules. An act of true chivalry happened when the son of Edward III, the 'Black Prince', served the captured King of France his dinner after defeating him at the Battle of Crécy.

A Knight's Training

From the age of seven a knight's son was sent to a nobleman's castle where he trained as a page. He learnt swordsmanship and riding. He had various chores and perhaps learnt to read and write. From the age of fourteen he became a squire and was attached to an individual knight. He looked after the knight's horse and weapons. He dressed him and joined him in battle, although he was rarely called to fight. At age twenty-one he was dubbed a knight. He took solemn vows to fear God, obey the Church, serve the King, live for honour, protect the weak, respect women and be chivalrous, generous and truthful.

Examples of 14th century great helms used in jousting tournaments

A Lady's Garter

The Order of the Garter was an order of knighthood begun by Edward III. He was dancing at a grand ball with the Countess of Salisbury, who he was in love with. As they danced one of her garters fell to the floor. Edward put it around his knee and rebuked the whispers from onlookers by saying, "Shame on him who thinks this shameful!" In Latin this translates into 'Honi soit qui mal y pense.' This became the motto for the order.

Above: In a pretty walled garden, knights and ladies share thoughts of love to the songs of a travelling minstrel. This romantic pursuit encouraged better treatment of women.

Right, a 13th century illuminated manuscript showing a jousting knight being killed before an audience of swooning ladies.

The knights are wearing helms, or large helmets, which reached down to the shoulders. One of the helmets is topped by a large heraldic crest. The helm alone could weigh over 10kg.

Did You Know?

The word 'chivalry' originally comes from the French word 'chevalerie' which means 'a body of horsemen'.

Life in a Castle

A castle was not just a place to be defended or attacked, it was a home and a centre for the administration of the surrounding estates. Many castles started life as a simple keep, but as their role changed and weapons developed, they became more complex in design.

Castles were placed strategically on high ground, or were surrounded by water for better defence. Some were built on rock so that the enemy could not destroy a wall by mining under it. Many were situated where an enemy might attack. For example, Dover Castle which was built to defend the English Channel from a French invasion. A few, like the beautifully preserved castle at Bodiam in East Sussex, were probably just status symbols. A lord, or baron had to ask the King for permission to build a castle. The King was not always keen on this, as it threatened his power. Castles in the north, or in Wales, were useful for defending border lands. Many castles were built by the King, such as those ordered by Edward I to keep the Welsh under control. They were looked after by a 'constable'.

Accommodation

The walls of rooms were sometimes plastered, covered with wood panels, or decorated with paintings or hanging tapestries. Belsay Castle was built in the 14th century and still has traces of elaborate paintings on its walls. A castle was a cold, dark place with open windows which had shutters, but not glass. The floors were wooden.

The great hall was the centre of activity. Here the lord, or baron, judged criminals and disputes over land and local taxes were paid here. The lord and his family had private rooms with guest rooms too. They had proper fireplaces, wash basins and toilets, or 'garderobes'. Garderobes were small rooms which extended over the moat with a chute, so that waste would fall into the water. They might be built into the wall and if there wasn't a moat the waste went down a chute and servants had to clean out the pit at the bottom! There was a kitchen, service rooms and often a chapel. Everyone drank beer, because water was not safe to drink, so there was also a brewery. The prison was in the keep where weapons and armour were stored.

How Many Soldiers Did Castles Have?

Keeping a large army was a very costly business. Large castles may have looked like they were defended by huge armies, but in reality most were garrisoned by only a handful of troops. The large walled areas were used for storage and could accommodate a visiting army. Often when attacked the castle residents would withdraw to the keep, which could easily be defended. It took an entire French army more than two weeks to defeat the defenders of Odiham Castle in 1216. It was manned by only three knights and ten sergeants! In 1252 Pembroke Castle had two mounted men-at-arms and ten foot soldiers. However, Rochester Castle had at least one hundred knights and soldiers when King John attacked it.

Lancaster Castle

Rochester Castle

Pick a Shape

Castles were built in all sorts of shapes as architects improved their defensive capabilities. Caerlaverock Castle in Scotland is triangular. Queenborough Castle in Kent is circular and surrounded by an outer circular wall and then a moat. Lancaster Castle in Lancashire had a gateway added with semi-octagonal shaped towers.

The keep at Dover Castle became a 'concentric' castle with the addition of two outer 'curtain' walls. Many Norman keeps were improved in this way as it was harder to use siege tactics against them. If the outer wall was attacked, the attackers could still be fired on from the inner wall. If part of an outer wall was captured it could be sectioned off. If attackers made it inside the first wall, they were trapped between it and the second wall, where they became easy targets.

Castle Under Siege!

1 ***The Ballista -*** *This was like a giant crossbow which fired a bolt, or dart. Impressive examples of siege engines are on permanent display at Caerphilly Castle in Wales.*

2 ***The Belfry -*** *This siege tower could be used to get a better firing position at defenders on the castle walls, or it could be moved up to the wall so that a drawbridge could be lowered for the attackers to cross. Rubble was used to create bridges over the moat.*

3 ***Battering Rams -*** *Used to smash walls or doors down and they were often covered with a shed, or 'penthouse' to protect the men inside.*

4 ***The Trebuchet -*** *This was a very heavy and slow siege weapon, but very effective at destroying castle walls. A ballast box provided the downforce on the lever, which catapulted huge stones at the defenders. Sometimes the putrid bodies of dead horses were fired to spread disease inside the castle.*

5 ***The Catapult -*** *This siege engine could hurl rocks at castle walls. In one crusade, the severed heads of soldiers were catapulted into a fortified city.*

Starvation and Disease

Another way of forcing a castle's occupants to surrender was to stop any supplies getting in and reinforcements arriving. This was achieved by completely surrounding the castle. The defenders were eventually forced to surrender, or face death by starvation and disease.

Mining

Miners dug a tunnel close to the wall, propping it up with wooden beams. A fire was then lit under the wall, burning the props and causing the wall to collapse.

The Church

The Church was well organised and very powerful in the middle ages. It had grown wealthy through donations from kings and nobility. The head of the Church in England, the Archbishop of Canterbury, was the most powerful man next to the King.

Christianity was very important to medieval society. Kings went on crusades to free Jerusalem from the clutches of the Muslims. People, rich and poor, went on pilgrimages to worship at the shrines of dead saints. The Church crowned kings and had its own laws and courts. It was the guardian of classical knowledge and began universities. It owned one third of all the land in England.

Church Organisation

The Pope, who was based in Rome, was the overall head of the Church. The Archbishop of Canterbury was next and then the Archbishop of York, who appointed bishops. The bishops were in charge of twenty-one dioceses, or regions of the kingdom. Each bishop was based in a cathedral and had a throne, or 'cathedra'. Each of these dioceses was divided into parishes and run by a priest based in a church. There were thousands of other workers in the Church too, called the 'clergy'.

Gothic Style

Many cathedrals and monasteries were built by the Normans in the Romanesque style, like Winchester, St Albans, Durham and Canterbury. Durham Cathedral, one of the finest, took just forty years to complete. Later they were added to in the more ornate 'Gothic' style from France, in the same way that castles were improved too. Wells and Salisbury Cathedrals are good examples of the English Gothic style. Later, this developed into the tall, slender 'Perpendicular' style, with much larger stained glass windows.

The Middleham Jewel is a 15th century gold pendant with a large sapphire. It was found near Middleham Castle, by a man with a metal detector. It is said to contain a piece of wood from The Cross, or some other relic associated with Christ. An inscription reveals that it was a charm used to protect the wearer from epilepsy.

Monks, Friars and Nuns

Monks lived in communities away from towns and villages. Originally the Order of St Benedict was the only order. Monks were supposed to be poor, unmarried and obedient, spending their time in work and prayer for God. In the 11th century new orders, such as the Cistercian order from France built new monasteries. They grew rich and wealthy by selling crops and producing wool from their huge flocks of sheep. Dominican Friars from Spain and Franciscan Friars from Italy lived and worked amongst the people, preaching and performing good works. Sometimes they came into conflict with the local clergy, or monks. Women could become nuns and live in a 'nunnery'. There were just as many orders of nuns, as there were monks and friars.

A Monks Life

Monks met up to nine times a day to pray. Some orders had shifts enabling them to spend all day and night in prayer. They grew their own food and made their own clothes, spending about six hours a day in manual labour. If they were good at copying manuscripts, they might be excused hard toil. They cared for the sick in their hospices, allowed nobles and the poor alike to stay as guests and taught boys to read and write. The abbot was in charge. He was a nobleman and often fought for the King.

Pilgrimages

People went on a pilgrimage at least once to ask for forgiveness for their sins, to give thanks for a happy event, or to pray for healing. They wore a badge to show where they had been, which they could buy at the shrine. Most pilgrims travelled on foot, taking a walking stick and a wide-brimmed hat to protect against the sun and rain. They visited the burial places of saints like Thomas Becket at Canterbury Cathedral, or St Cuthbert at Durham Cathedral. Sometimes shrines had holes in them, so pilgrims could touch the bones. The Pope made someone a saint if they had died heroically, or had lived sacrificially for Jesus Christ.

Canterbury Cathedral

Canterbury Cathedral was built by Archbishop LanFranc and was later added to in the Gothic style. Like many cathedrals, it was run by a community of monks who lived in a monastery to the north of the cathedral. The shrine of Thomas Becket made it one of the leading places of pilgrimage in Europe.

The cathedral was added to through the ages. Look at the illustrations below and see if you can see how it has grown.

1 *The stained glass windows filled the 25 metre high nave with light. They depict scenes from the life of Jesus and Old Testament stories.*

2 *The nave was re-built in the late 14th century. It did not originally have benches, so there was plenty of room for pilgrims and worshippers.*

3 *The central bell tower, Bell Harry, was the last part to be built in the late 15th century. It is over 75 metres high.*

4 *The quire is where the monks sang psalms and services were held daily here, but only the clergy could attend them.*

5 *The Trinity Chapel was built shortly after Becket's martyrdom in 1170 and it is where his shrine is housed.*

6 *The Corona, built at the same time as the Trinity Chapel. Archbishops are enthroned in St Augustine's chair here.*

Did You Know?

Geoffrey Chaucer wrote a long poem called 'The Canterbury Tales'. The poem follows a group of pilgrims who are on their way to Becket's shrine at Canterbury. He wrote it in the dialect of London and south-east England. Its popularity helped to establish it as the standard language of the nation.

Craftsmen and Merchants

As travelling craftsmen and merchants had to find places to stay during the winter they gathered in small communities, which grew into thriving towns. The successful English wool trade also encouraged town growth in centres of the cloth industry.

Transport by river and sea was better than by road and towns like Bristol became very important. 'Sea-coal' found on beaches, and mined coal was brought by ship from Newcastle to London. Places like Leeds and Bradford grew as their rivers powered watermills for the cloth industry. Carts were used for transport and covered about twenty to thirty miles a day.

The Wool Trade

English wool was the best in Europe and from the 1300's English cloth was exported in vast quantities. After shearing the sheep the wool was combed and spun into yarn using a weighted spindle. Then it was woven by women into cloth on a loom and pounded in water at a mill to thicken it and remove the grease. Finally, it was stretched on frames to dry and then it was dyed in dyers workshops.

Guilds

As early as the 11th century, craftsmen and merchants banded together to form associations called 'guilds'. They made laws to protect their trade. Eventually the guilds became very powerful and helped to create a new middle class, some of whom become nobles. It was this wealthy class that financed much of the cathedral building in the late middle ages. Guilds could control the price and quality of their products and stop competition.

In Derby the guild of cloth dyers were granted a law which stated that 'no one should dye cloth within ten leagues of Derby, except in Derby'. There were all kinds of guilds, from cooks to artists.
To join a guild and become a master craftsman, young boys served as apprentices for seven years and paid a membership fee. The guilds built splendid meeting halls, or 'Guildhalls', like those in York and London.

Types of Craftsmen

Some craftsmen were blacksmiths who produced iron tools, buckets, barrel hoops, cauldrons, pans, knives, candle holders, hinges, padlocks, nails, weapons and armour. Bronzesmiths made church bells and jewellery. Tanners and leather workers produced belts, purses, harnesses, jugs and bottles. Glassmakers created small bottles and glass for church windows and later windows for houses. Potters made clay pots, roof tiles and floor tiles for churches, palaces, castles and grand houses. There were carpenters and thatchers who built houses. Coopers skilfully made air-tight barrels, bending the oak into shape by steaming it. Stonemasons built beautiful Gothic cathedrals and plasterers and plumbers worked in lead. Armourers, painters, sculptors, furniture makers, shipbuilders and tailors were all highly skilled craftsmen.

Mining

Mining was an important industry. Stone was mined for castles, cathedrals and houses. Lead from the north of England was used on rooves, water pipes and small ornaments, such as pilgrim badges (see page 9). Tin and lead were combined to make pewter. Iron ore was heated in furnaces, smelted and hammered into a variety of products.

Money and Shops

Money was used to buy goods and was essential for trade, but there were different measures of gold and silver. Some merchants and traders were dishonest, so Henry I was the first king to set uniform standards throughout the Kingdom.

Shops did not have big windows as they do today. They were often one room in the front of a house with a workshop behind.

A 15th century merchant ship based on one found in Newport. It was over 25 metres in length.

A Medieval Port

A cargo of French wine in barrels is being unloaded from a merchant ship. Other imports included vegetables, such as cabbages, garlic and onions from Europe. Furs and wood for bows from the Baltic and lace from Flanders, which was north-eastern France and Belgium. Building stone came from Normandy, timber from Scandinavia, wax for candles and canvas from the Holy Roman Empire in central Europe. Enamelled glass from Syria, rugs, sugar cane, figs, raisins and spices from the east. Popular exports from England were bales of wool, coal, lead, tin, pewterware, live sheep, bacon, butter, cheese and alabaster carvings.

Did You Know?

Medieval English wool has never been surpassed in quality. The white robes worn by the Pope today are still made from English wool.

Did You Know?

Merchant vessels were sometimes seized in times of war and used for military purposes, which is why they often had ramparts like castles built on the front and rear.

Towns and Villages

A Saxon village with its thatched cottages, church and lord's manor changed little after the Norman invasion. As trade with Europe and beyond increased, towns started to flourish.

Farm Life

Villeins worked strips of land for the local baron and themselves. Below villeins came the 'bordars' who had less land and did not own livestock. Farm work was tough, except for ploughing, which was done with oxen. Sheep provided wool, meat and cheese made from their milk. Poultry produced eggs and feathers for arrows. Wheat, barley, rye, oats and peas were grown, while some fields were left fallow every other year. Wheat was ground in the manor's watermill. The manor might also have a vineyard. A 'tithe' of food was paid to the church and compensation paid to the baron if someone died, or if a girl left after marrying.

Country Food

The Church banned meat on Fridays and Holy days. Most people couldn't afford it except during the slaughtering season, so fish caught in the local river was popular. Dinner might be a vegetable stew, dark bread and ale, with bread and eggs for supper. The rich had white bread and wine.

Farmhouses

In the west and north of Britain ordinary houses were built in stone, otherwise timber framed houses with wattle and daub walls were the most common. A family would live in one end and keep their animals in the other end, which helped to keep the house warm and smelly!
By the 15th century some farmers became rich due to the booming wool trade and were able to build better houses, some of which survive today.

The Manor House

The manor house, where the baron and his household lived, became the centre of community life in medieval times. Villagers met there for legal and administrative purposes. Some manor houses were built in brick, an idea from northern Europe. In war-torn areas such as Wales and Scotland it was the castle which dominated daily life.

Town Life

Only ten per cent of the population lived in towns, which were noisy, dirty, cramped places. Rubbish was thrown into open drains and animals were kept in yards next to the houses. People rose at daybreak and a bell announced the opening of the town gates. When a curfew bell sounded at night people barred their doors and went to bed.

Town Houses

By the 13th century rich merchants could afford two-storey houses. They had lots of furniture and slept in wooden beds with linen sheets. They even had glass windows. People used outside toilets, or an indoor toilet which emptied into a pit in the cellar. They washed in public bathhouses.

Town Food

Most food was boiled, or roasted on a spit in a kitchen, or sometimes in the yard to reduce the risk of fire. Water came from the river, a well or street seller. Servants took ingredients to the local baker, or pie-maker to make pastries and pies. Eels, cod, herring, ham, fruit and cheese were eaten and herbs and spices were used in cooking.

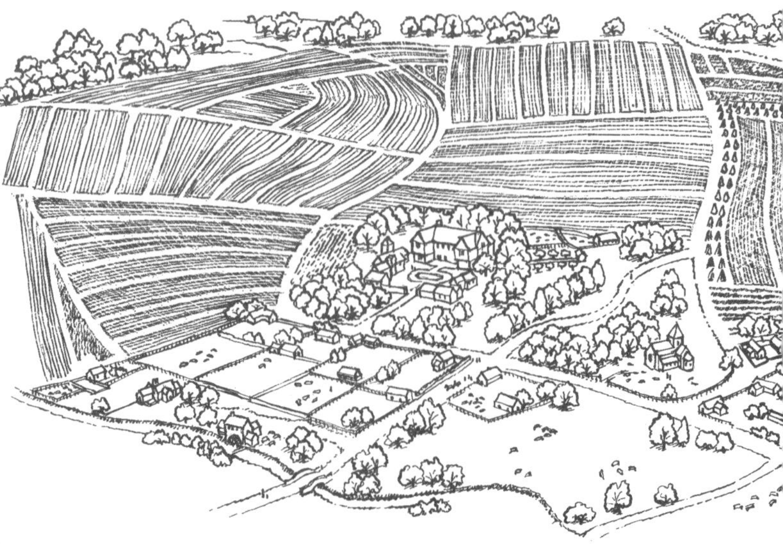

A typical 14th century manor with a manor house in the centre and land reserved for the baron's use. It is surrounded by arable land, a village with its church, pasture land in the foreground, sheep folds and a mill on the river. The priest cultivated a plot of his own land.

Market Day

Villages and towns had markets once a week. For a small tax you could sell your wares on a piece of ground, or set up a stall. Some markets attracted international merchants. It was a place to gossip and watch the street entertainers. Important business was done in the stone market-cross shown here, several have survived in places like Salisbury and Chichester. People could buy vegetables, butter, salt, fish, live animals, penny pies and kitchenware. It was also a favourite place for pickpockets and beggars. Religious plays were performed in the church, or on carts and by the 1400's actors put on morality plays about good versus evil.

Fairs

Rich and poor went to the fairs to see minstrels, jugglers, fire-eaters, sword swallowers, acrobats, clowns and fortune tellers. You could also gamble on cock-fights, wrestling, or bear-baiting. A typical fair might last three weeks.

A Peasant's Calendar

Spring - Rain softened the land for ploughing and sowing crops. Dogs and children with slings scared the birds away from the crop seeds. Easter was a time of festivities. After the May Day celebrations buildings, fences, hedgerows and drainage ditches were repaired.
Summer - Time for sheep shearing and haymaking. Everyone helped to harvest the crops in September. The baron provided pork, chicken, cabbages, eggs, cheese and apples for the harvesters.
Autumn - Firewood was gathered from the baron's woods and nuts for the pigs were shaken from trees. Many farm animals were killed and preserved with salt. This saved on winter fodder and provided food for the winter.
Winter - Much feasting, churchgoing and festivities ended with the twelve days of Christmas. The baron served a big meal for all of the villagers.

Would you rather live in the town or in a village? Discuss the advantages and disadvantages of both. Page 9 describes the life of a monk. Would you prefer to be a monk, or a villein in the middle ages?

Did You Know?

By 1300 England had a population of about 4 million people, but there were more than 15 million sheep!

Norman Kings and Queens

William the Conqueror was a strong ruler who increased the power of the monarchy and united England. He brought the country up to date with European society. He died in France in 1087 when his horse stumbled in a burning street during a military campaign.

William II 1087-1100
Like his father, William 'Rufus' was an excellent soldier. He gained control of most of Normandy from his older brother Robert. He may have been called 'Rufus' because of his red beard or face! He was unpopular in England and had to stop a rebellion against his rule. He was mysteriously killed whilst hunting in the New Forest. He never married and had no heir, so when his brother Henry heard the news of his death he seized the throne, whilst his brother Robert was on a crusade in the Holy Land.

Henry I 1100-1135
Robert fought Henry in 1106, but he was defeated. Henry took Normandy and united it with England. Robert was imprisoned, but escaped and Henry re-captured him and had his eyes burnt out. Henry governed England well and introduced new laws, which were the forerunner of the Magna Carta. He named his daughter Matilda as his successor.

England Ruled by a Woman!
The barons did not want to be ruled by a woman and didn't like Matilda's husband, Geoffrey of Anjou. He was nicknamed 'Plantagenet' after a flower he adopted as his emblem. So Henry's nephew Stephen was crowned king, breaking an oath he had made to protect Matilda's rights. England was plunged into civil war as the barons' power went unchecked by the new weak king. Some barons sided with Matilda. In 1141 she captured the King, but she was never crowned queen. She was finally defeated and fled to Normandy, never to return.

Matilda the Escape Artist!

The same year that Matilda escaped from captivity in Oxford, she escaped from another castle by disguising herself as a corpse and being carried out for burial!

Stephen 1135-1153
Stephen was well-liked, but he failed to control the barons and in 1153, Henry, the son of Matilda and Geoffrey Plantagenet, landed in England to claim the throne. He was very powerful, having married Eleanor of Aquitaine, who ruled over a large part of France. However, Henry could not beat Stephen, but he did manage to persuade Stephen to make him heir to the throne. Stephen was the last of the Norman kings when he died.

Henry II 1154-1189
Henry II needed to regain control of England from the powerful barons. He travelled around England and France destroying the castles that the barons had built without royal permission. He restored the legal system of Trial by Jury, begun by his grandfather Henry I. This replaced the barbaric Trial by Combat and Trial by Ordeal. Judges were assisted by a jury of twelve men and if found guilty, defendants had the right to appeal to a royal court.

Henry was helped in these reforms by his friend Thomas Becket, who he made his top advisor, or Chancellor. Thomas was a brave soldier who once led 700 knights into battle against the King of France.

Becket Made Archbishop of Canterbury
Henry's reforms brought him into conflict with the Church, so he made his friend, Thomas Becket, Archbishop of Canterbury in 1162. Becket warned him that this might strain their friendship. Becket defended the Church's position and resigned his post as Chancellor, angering Henry who had him accused of treason.

Create a 'coat of arms' for your family. It might be inspired by an activity you enjoy or an animal you like. It should include a shield topped by a helmet. The shield could be held by animals, or people either side. Underneath the coat of arms write your family motto.

Arms and Armour

By the early 13th century most knights wore helmets with face protection.

Armour continued to develop and in the late 13th century plate armour was added to the mail coat. Knights wore 'surcoats' over their armour, which displayed their coat of arms.

By the 15th century knights wore full suits of interlocking plate armour, curved to deflect arrows and sword thrusts.

Horse armour had been in use since the 13th century and included a coat of mail for the body and neck, or 'trapper', large metal or leather plates and metal 'chanfrons' for the head.

The War of the Roses saw the introduction of cannon and handguns. Burgundian mercenaries brought multiple-barrelled artillery with them. Although they inflicted serious casualties they were slow to re-load.

The longbow was used to great effect in many battles, particularly against the French knights during the 'Hundred Years' War'. Within 45 metres the heavy arrows could penetrate shields and armour. Archers trained from boyhood to master the fearsome pull of the bowstring. Crossbowmen did not need to train as hard, or be as strong as a longbowman owing to the crossbow's design. It fired deadly bolts, which could also pierce plate armour, but its range was shorter and it was slower to re-load.

Foot soldiers were usually recruited by the local lord and wore a variety of armour, including mail hauberks, coats of plate armour riveted inside cloth or leather and quilted, or stuffed cloth jackets called 'gambesons'. The soldier opposite carries a pole arm, which could be as long as 4.5 metres and was used to topple a knight from his horse.

The Plantagenet Kings

Thomas Becket fled to France. In 1170 Henry crowned his son king to ensure his succession to the throne, but he did not ask Becket to crown him. However, the two made up their differences and Becket returned to England.

Becket had all those who took part in the coronation of Henry's son excommunicated, which meant unless they repented they were going to hell! When the King found out, he is said to have exclaimed, "Who will rid me of this meddlesome priest?"

The King is Whipped by Eighty Monks!

Four knights took the King at his word and travelled to Canterbury Cathedral and murdered Becket. Many miracles were reported after his death and the Pope made Becket a saint. Pilgrims flocked to Canterbury. Henry's own wife and sons rebelled against him and the King of Scotland declared war! People saw this as God's judgement on the King. Henry went to Becket's shrine with other pilgrims and was whipped by eighty monks as penance. The King of Scotland was captured and all but one of Henry's sons' stepped into line. Henry's son, Richard, rebelled with French help and Henry died a broken man.

Richard I 1189-1199

Richard 'The Lionheart' spent his reign on crusades to the Holy Land, or defending his French lands, staying less than a year in England. In fact, he spoke French and couldn't speak a word of English! His father had set up an efficient government, which coped with his long absence. Richard appointed William Longchamp, the Bishop of Ely to govern England, but his remaining brother, John, took control, backed by many of the barons. Richard was killed by a crossbow bolt, while laying siege to a French castle.

WHAT A WAY TO GO!

Edward I devised a nasty way to execute traitors. William Wallace was pulled through London on a sledge. He was hanged until half dead, released from the noose and his stomach cut open and his digestive system pulled out and burned. Then he was beheaded and his body cut into four parts! His head was stuck on a pole on London Bridge and his body parts were displayed as a warning to rebels in four towns in the north.

John 1199-1216

John was not popular and he probably murdered his young nephew Arthur. He made heavy demands on the barons and Church to finance his wars with France. He lost almost all of his French lands. Tradition has it that the barons swore an oath on St Edmund's Day 1214 at the High Altar of the Great Abbey of St Edmunds Bury to give John a list of demands, the Magna Carta. This they did at Runnymede near Windsor. John did not stick to this agreement and during the civil war which resulted he became sick and died.

Henry III 1216-1272

Henry chose his French friends as advisors, which angered the barons. Led by Simon de Montfort, they demanded he consult them. The King agreed, but broke his word and war followed. The barons defeated Henry at the Battle of Lewes in 1264. De Montfort ruled England with Henry's son, Prince Edward, held as a hostage. He called a Parliament and allowed common people, as well as nobles, to have their say. However, Prince Edward escaped and defeated Simon de Montfort.

Edward I 1272-1307

Edward 'longshanks' was a very tall man. He had sixteen children by his first wife and when she died, he had three children with his second wife. He defeated the Prince of Wales, Llewellyn ap Gruffyd and organised Wales into shires like England. He built many castles to control the Welsh, such as Caernarvon, Harlech and Conwy.

After the death of the Scottish King, Alexander, he tried to seize Scotland. The Scots, led by William Wallace and a French nobleman, Robert de Brus, or Robert the Bruce, rebelled. Wallace's untrained army defeated a superior English army at Stirling Bridge, but Wallace was later captured and executed. Bruce crowned himself king, but did not have the support of the Scottish nobles and had to go into hiding.

The Murder of Thomas Becket

Four knights crossed the English Channel and rode to Becket's house in Canterbury. They told Becket, "The King commands that you shall leave this realm." The Archbishop refused and the knights stormed out to put on their armour.

Staff hurried Becket from his house to the cathedral telling him it was time for prayers. In the cathedral, Becket's men bolted the doors, but he ordered them to unlock them, as it was a church, not a castle. The knights burst in, swords drawn, shouting, "Where is the traitor?". All of Becket's staff ran away except for Edward Grim, who put his arm out to stop the blow from a sword. It cut his arm to the bone and gashed Becket's head. Becket fell to the ground and one of the knights killed him.

YUCK!

When they removed Becket's bloodstained clothes, they found he was wearing a hair shirt next to his skin. It was alive with lice and worms and he must have been in constant agony. People saw this as proof that he had lived a holy life.

Lancastrian and Yorkist Kings

Edward I died on his way to start a military campaign in Scotland. His son Edward, who had been made Prince of Wales at Caernarvon Castle, became king. He went to Scotland with a huge army, but he was defeated at Bannockburn in 1314 by Bruce's tiny force.

Edward II 1307-1327
Edward II was unpopular because of his choice of male favourites. His wife Isabella, a powerful French noblewoman, invaded England with an army. Edward was imprisoned and murdered.

Edward III 1327-1377
Through his mother Isabella, Edward III had a strong claim to the French throne. With the help of his son Edward, the 'Black Prince', he defeated the French at Crécy in 1346 and at Poitiers in 1356. During the 'Hundred Years War' he lost his French gains, quarrelled with Parliament and the Black Prince died in 1376. Edward died soon after. During his reign the 'Black Death' swept through Britain several times, killing one in four people.

Richard II and the Poll Tax Riots 1377-1399
The Black Prince's son was ten when he became king, so John of Gaunt and twelve other men governed England. Instead of taxing property to support the war with France, a new tax on heads was introduced called the 'poll tax'. There was a lot of anger about the tax in the south-east. In 1381 peasants stormed London, led by Wat Tyler, but the Mayor of London attacked and wounded Tyler. At this dangerous moment the fourteen year old king bravely stepped forward and offered to become the rebels' new leader. The crowds left and although some rebels were hanged most were pardoned.

The Lancastrian Kings: Henry IV 1399-1413
When John of Gaunt died Richard took his land. John's banished son, Henry Bolingbroke, sailed to England to reclaim them. Henry was popular and Parliament made him Richard's successor. Richard was imprisoned and starved to death in 1400. The Duke of Northumberland and his son Henry Percy, or 'Hotspur', opposed the King and were helped by Owen Glendower, the leader of a rebellion in Wales. Henry put down the revolt and Hotspur was killed at the Battle of Shrewsbury. He suffered rebellions for the rest of his reign.

Henry V 1413-1422
Henry V united the nobles and renewed his claim to the French throne. He won a famous victory at Agincourt, but later became ill and died in France.

The Wars of the Roses
Henry VI suffered from bouts of insanity. During the first one Richard, Duke of York, who had a strong claim to the throne, was appointed Protector of England. When Henry recovered, his French Queen Margaret persuaded him to dismiss Richard, who gathered an army and defeated Henry in 1455. Richard and the Yorkists adopted a white rose as their badge, while Henry and the Lancastrians chose a red rose. Civil war followed. Richard was killed in 1460, but Margaret and the Lancastrians were beaten and Richard's son Edward IV became king. Henry was captured and Margaret fled to France.

Warwick the 'Kingmaker'
The Earl of Warwick had helped the Yorkists, but he became angry when Edward married a Lancastrian. He rebelled, but had to flee to France. He later returned and marched to London with Henry. This time Edward had to escape, but he later defeated the Lancastrians at Barnet, where Warwick was killed. Margaret was captured, her son and many Lancastrians were killed and Henry died in the Tower of London. Edward was succeeded by his twelve year old son Edward V in 1483, but his uncle seized the throne and became Richard III. He imprisoned Edward V and his brother Richard in the Tower of London. The 'Princes in the Tower' mysteriously died. Another Lancastrian, Henry Tudor, fought and defeated Richard at the Battle of Bosworth in 1485. Henry then became Henry VII and married Edward's daughter, uniting the houses of Lancaster and York, beginning the Tudor age.

Owain Glyn Dwr, or Owen Glendower was the last Welshman to hold the title of Prince of Wales. He did rebel against English rule but he was never caught.

The Battle of Agincourt 1415

Henry's army, depleted by war and disease, was probably only 900 men-at-arms and 5,000 longbowmen. They faced a French army of around 20,000 cavalry and 4-6,000 crossbowmen and archers. The English archers were placed on the flanks with a few in the centre. It had rained heavily the night before and on the morning of the 25th October both armies faced each other across a narrow stretch of land. No one made the first move, so Henry ordered his tiny force forward just beyond the range of French archers. His longbowmen dug their sharpened stakes into the ground at an angle to protect them from a cavalry charge. This was the first time they had used stakes for defence. Then they fired at the French. Some dismounted men-at-arms charged at them, but were cut down by a wave of arrows. The French were so tightly packed that they could not easily use their weapons and their heavy armour bogged them down in the mud. However, the English were beaten back as the French line was reinforced. The English lightly armed longbowmen and men-at-arms had the advantage in the muddy, cramped conditions and they rushed upon the mass of dead horses and writhing bodies and slaughtered the French with clubs, swords and billhooks. They captured many nobles to ransom them and stole what armour and weapons they fancied. Henry fought bravely and at one point cut his way through the enemy to drag his wounded brother to safety. The English lost a few hundred men, but the French suffered thousands of casualties.

MURDER MYSTERY

Richard III has had a bad rap ever since Shakespeare described him as a wicked hunchback. He was accused of murdering the princes in the Tower. The princes had been declared illegitimate heirs and the throne was offered to Richard. Some bones of two boys were discovered hidden in the Tower of London and tests indicate they may be of royal blood. In 1502 Sir James Tyrell supposedly confessed to their murder and was beheaded. Find out about the disappearance of the princes. Discuss what you think might have happened.

Giant Medieval Word Search

K	E	G	A	U	I	D	R	A	W	D	E	A	L	S	Z	A	M	O	B
T	E	N	O	T	H	O	M	A	S	B	E	C	K	E	T	I	V	A	A
R	T	E	A	T	E	V	L	E	R	A	W	N	A	I	D	A	T	H	T
A	E	M	P	G	U	E	L	R	A	V	I	D	A	D	T	T	U	T	T
E	M	E	T	E	U	R	I	O	R	E	S	T	L	K	L	K	G	Z	L
H	Q	L	E	C	T	C	S	N	E	M	U	E	I	E	O	E	A	B	E
N	E	B	O	N	D	A	T	T	I	R	H	N	O	O	S	E	R	Y	O
O	R	O	U	L	S	S	A	R	P	A	G	F	B	R	N	K	D	A	F
I	S	N	O	U	L	T	G	S	M	A	H	Y	A	R	N	N	E	M	B
L	N	R	I	D	S	L	A	J	R	A	A	T	I	I	X	Y	R	O	O
E	A	A	S	S	I	E	E	T	S	D	E	G	G	N	A	R	O	D	S
H	M	A	S	P	C	W	H	T	S	B	Y	H	N	O	S	A	B	N	W
T	R	G	E	A	E	U	I	E	I	R	T	U	A	I	O	N	E	A	O
D	O	I	D	L	R	N	M	R	L	S	E	L	U	A	T	O	S	L	R
R	N	N	C	N	G	O	T	A	O	N	E	C	U	T	G	S	A	Y	T
A	I	C	A	S	D	I	V	U	P	O	P	E	I	P	N	G	U	L	H
H	U	O	S	R	Q	I	T	I	Q	A	E	S	E	A	A	E	G	O	E
C	S	U	T	E	H	P	L	A	N	T	A	G	E	N	E	T	N	H	J
I	E	R	L	C	T	U	Q	I	V	E	M	E	D	I	E	V	A	L	T
R	O	T	E	L	T	S	A	C	H	G	U	O	R	O	B	R	A	C	S

Medieval
Knights
Noblemen
Holy Land
Battle of Bosworth

Chivalry
Plantagenet
Castle
Battle of Hastings
Harold

Normans
Domesday Book
Scarborough Castle
Jousting
Dover Castle

Edward I
Garderobes
Catapult
Middleham Jewel
Thomas Becket

Pilgrims
Pope
Richard the Lionheart
Agincourt
Keep